WORKBOOK

Real-Life English

A COMPETENCY–BASED ESL PROGRAM FOR ADULTS

Program Consultants

Jayme Adelson-Goldstein
North Hollywood Learning Center
North Hollywood, California

Patricia De Hesus-Lopez
Texas A & M University
Kingsville, Texas

Julia Collins
Los Angeles Unified School District
El Monte-Rosemead Adult School
El Monte, California

Federico Salas-Isnardi
Houston Community College
Adult Literacy Programs
Houston, Texas

Else V. Hamayan
Illinois Resource Center
Des Plaines, Illinois

Connie Villaruel
El Monte-Rosemead Adult School
El Monte, California

Kent Heitman
Carver Community Middle School
Delray Beach, Florida

Wei-hua (Wendy) Wen
Adult & Continuing Education
New York City Board of Education
New York, New York

STECK-VAUGHN
C O M P A N Y
ELEMENTARY • SECONDARY • ADULT • LIBRARY

ACKNOWLEDGMENTS

Staff Credits:

Executive Editor ♦ Ellen Lehrburger
Senior Editor ♦ Tim Collins
Design Manager ♦ Richard Balsam
Cover Design ♦ Richard Balsam
Photo Editor ♦ Margie Foster

Photo Credits:

Cover: James Minor, Cooke Photographics (title); © Randal Alhadeff–p.49;
© Michelle Bridwell–p.9, 16; © Patti Gilliam–p.65; © Stephanie Huebinger–p.17, 33;
James Minor–p.1, 4, 6; © Park Street–p.73a; © Daniel Thompson Photography–p.25,
41, 57, 63a, 63c, 63e; © Mary Pat Waldron–p.63b, 63d, 63f; Sandy Wilson–p.18.

Additional Photography by:
P.73a © Tommy Dodson/Unicorn; p.73b © Betts Anderson/Unicorn; p.73c Dick Young/Unicorn.

Illustration Credits:

The Ivy League of Artists, Inc.

Additional Illustration by:
Scott Bieser–p.19 (flag); Tami Crabb–p.30; David Griffin–p.7, 8, 44 (bills);
John Harrison–p.19c, 19d, 44 (coins); John Hartwell–p.9-16; Lyle Miller–p.26, 51, 55.

Electronic Production:

International Electronic Publishing Center, Inc.

CONTENTS

To The Student And The Teacher

Every unit of this Workbook has ten exercises. There are one or more exercises for each section of the Student Book. Use this chart to find the exercise(s) for each section. For example, after the "Talk It Over" page, do Exercise 3. After the "Structure Base" pages, do Exercises 7A, 7B, 7C, etc.

Student Book Section	Workbook Exercise
Unit Opener	1
Starting Out	2
Talk It Over	3
Word Bank	4A, 4B, 4C, etc.
Listening	5
Reading	6
Structure Base	7A, 7B, 7C, etc.
Write It Down	8
One To One	9
Extension	10

Personal Communication

1. Complete the sentences.

✔

from   last   name   you

1. My first _____name_____ is Marta.

2. My _____ name is Cantu.

3. I'm _____ Nicaragua.

4. How about _____ ?

2. Answer the questions. Write about yourself.

➤ Where are you from?

● _____

➤ What language do you speak?

● _____

➤ Where do you live?

● _____

3. Complete the dialog. ✔

from   hello   language   meet   nice   speak

➤ Hi, I'm a new student.

● <u>Hello</u>. I'm new, too. My name's Mei.

➤ _____ to meet you, Mei. My name is Marta.

● Nice to _____ you, Marta. Where are you _____?

➤ I'm from Nicaragua. How about you?

● I'm from China.

➤ What _____ do you speak?

● Chinese. What language do you _____?

➤ I speak Spanish.

4A. Write the number.

 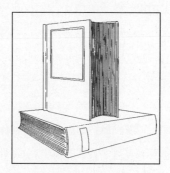 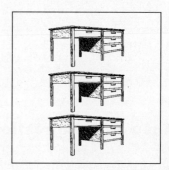

1. <u>five</u> pens   2. _____ books   3. _____ desks

4. _____ pencils   5. _____ chairs   6. _____ board

4B. Find the words.

✔
ADDRESS
CITY
NAME
STATE
NATIONALITY

A D R G Y H E W T (N A M E) T

N A T I O N A L I T Y E T W

V E S T A T E R Y C I T Y I

X S R T G Q S T U K I U Y D

S A W A D D R E S S Q R T H

4C. What are they? Write the letters.

___b___ 1. (512)   a. ZIP Code

_____ 2. 60068   ✔ b. area code

_____ 3. 715-32-5117   c. telephone number

_____ 4. 555-4801   d. Social Security number

4D. Answer the questions. Write about yourself.

1. Where do you live? _____

2. What is your area code? _____

3. What is your telephone number? _____

4. What language do you speak? _____

5. What is your Social Security number? _____

5. Look at the card. Read it. Answer the questions.

1. What's her last name? _____ Garcia _____

2. What's her first name? _____

3. What's her address? _____

_____

4. What's her ZIP Code? _____

5. Where's she from? _____

Maria Garcia (Mexico)
123 Green Street
Los Angeles, CA 91251

6. Look and read.

MORE NEW STUDENTS

Pablo Garcia and Cynthia Wang are new students at City Center.
Pablo is from Mexico.
He lives in Miami.
His address is 456 Green Street.
His ZIP Code is 33187.

Cynthia is from China.
She's Chinese.
She lives in Miami, too.
Her address is 715 New Street.
Her ZIP Code is 33151.

Write yes or no.

yes 1. Pablo Garcia is from Mexico.

_no_ 2. His address is 715 New Street.

_____ 3. His ZIP Code is 33151.

_____ 4. Cynthia Wang is from Mexico.

_____ 5. She lives in China.

_____ 6. Her address is 715 New Street.

7A. Complete the sentences.

I am		a new student.
He	is	
She		

We	are new students.
You	
They	

1. Many students _are_ in our class. We _are_ from many countries.

2. My name _is_ Marta. I _am_ from Mexico.

3. Jean and Marie _are_ from Canada. They _are_ Canadian.

4. Nyugen _____ from Vietnam. He _____ Vietnamese.

5. Tuyet _____ Vietnamese, too. She _____ a new student.

6. Pablo _____ a new student, too. He _____ from El Salvador.

7B. Change the words.

I	+	am	=	I'm
he	+	is	=	he's
she	+	is	=	she's

we	+	are	=	we're
you	+	are	=	you're
they	+	are	=	they're

1. **They are** in school.   _They're_ in school.

2. **We are** English students.   _____ English students.

3. **She is** from Africa.   _____ from Africa.

4. **You are** new in school.   _____ new in school.

5. **He is** the teacher.   _____ the teacher.

6. **I am** from Haiti.   _____ from Haiti.

7C. Complete the sentences.

I	my
he	his
she	her
we	our
you	your
they	their

My last name is Bueno.

1. Hello. ___My___ name is Nadia. I'm from Russia.

2. This is my friend. She's from Russia, too. _____ name is Elena.

3. We're in the same English class. _____ class is nice.

4. _____ teacher is good. She's from Chicago.

   _____ name is Kim.

5. Boris and Peter are in a different class.

   _____ teacher is very good. He's from Los Angeles.

   _____ name is Bill.

6

7D. Read the answers. Write the questions.

Where are	you	from?
	they	
Where's	she	
	he	

I'm	from Korea
She's	
He's	
We're	
They're	

➤ <u>What's your name?</u>

● My name is Marta Torres.

➤ _____

● My address is 704 Brown Street, Miami, Florida.

➤ _____

● My ZIP Code is 33188.

➤ _____

● I'm from Nicaragua.

8. Complete the form. Write about yourself.

**EMPLOYMENT APPLICATION
DALLAS COMPUTER COMPANY**

Name:_____
          Last   First   Middle

Address:_____
         Number   Street   Apartment

City:_____ State:_____ ZIP Code:_____

Social Security or Other Identification Number:_____

Native Language:_____

Telephone Number:_____
        (Area Code)   Number

9. Mrs. Smith needs a new library card.
You work in the library.
What do you ask Mrs. Smith?
Write the questions.

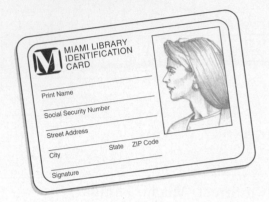

1. What's your first name?

2. _____

3. _____

4. _____

5. _____

10. Complete the dialog. ✔

| fine   hi   nice   see   you |

➤ Hello, Tron.

● ___Hi___, Mei. How are _____?

➤ _____, thanks. How about you, Tron?

● Fine, thanks. How do you like New York?

➤ It's nice.

● Well, nice to _____ you, Mei.

➤ Thanks, Tron. _____ to see you, too.

2 Our Community

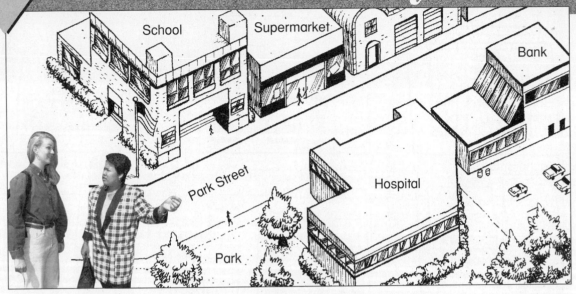

I. Complete the dialog.

✔

| left   supermarket   where |

➤ <u>Where</u> are you going?

● I'm going to the _____ on Park Street.

➤ Which way is it?

● Go _____ on this street. It's not very far.

2. Look at the map.
Complete the sentences.
Write the letters.

1. The school is across from the __b__.   a. bank

2. The _____ is next to the school.   ✔ b. park

3. The hospital is between the park and the _____.   c. hospital

4. The bank is next to the _____.   d. supermarket

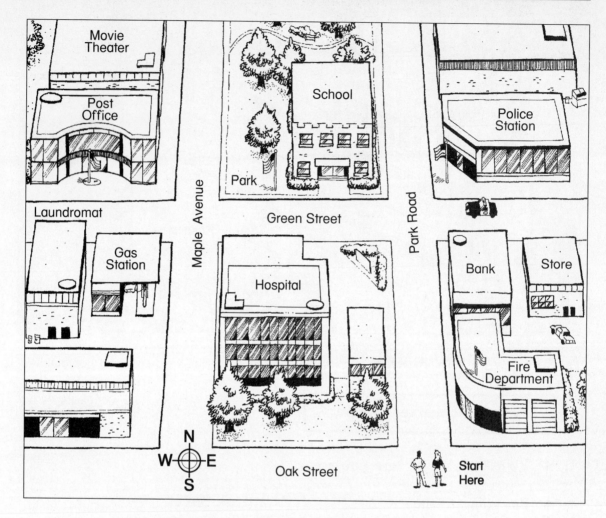

3. Look at the map. Complete the dialogs.

✔

south street where's

➤ Excuse me. ___Where's___ the hospital?

● The hospital is _____ of the park.

➤ Where?

● It's on Green _____, one block south of the park.

across avenue post office

■ Excuse me. Where's the _____?

● It's on Maple _____, _____ from the park.

4A. Write the letters.

1. ga_s_ s_t_ati_o_n

2. p__st o__fice

3. __ir__ t__uck

4. s__or__

5. p__lice ca__

6. fi__e

4B. Complete the directions to the movie theater. Use the map on page 10.

✔

left   north   right   turn   walk   west

From Oak Street and Park Road, _____walk_____ north on Park Road.

Go one block to Green Street. _____ left.

Go one block _____ to Maple Avenue.

Turn _____.

The movie theater is one block _____.

It's on the _____, next to the post office.

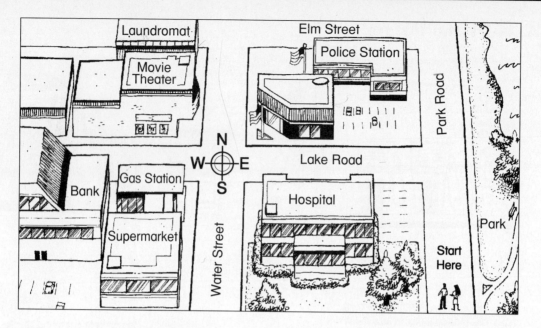

5. Complete the dialog.

✔

| movie theater   next to   street |

➤ I'm going to the _____movie theater_____.

● What movie theater?

➤ The movie theater on Water _____.

● Is it next to the hospital?

➤ No, it isn't. It's _____ the laundromat.

6. Read the notice.
Follow the directions. Draw a line on the map in 5.

Public Meeting
September 1, 4:00 P.M.
at City School

Directions:
From the park, go one block north on Park Road. Turn left on Lake Road. Walk one block to Water Street. City School is on the right, on the corner of Lake Road and Water Street.

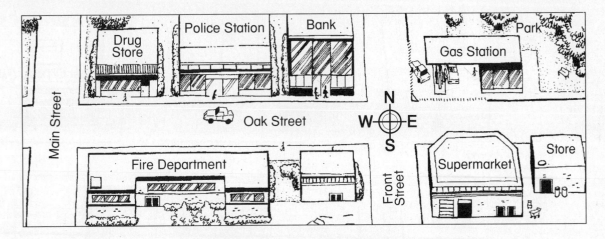

7A. Look at the map. Answer the questions.

Am	I	on Main Street?
Is	he	
	she	
	it	
Are	we	
	you	
	they	

Yes,	I am.	
	he	is.
	she	
	it	
	we	are.
	you	
	they	

No,	I'm not.	
	he	isn't.
	she	
	it	
	we	aren't.
	you	
	they	

1. Is the bank on Main Street? _No, it isn't._

2. Is the police station on Oak Street? _____

3. Are the drug store and
   supermarket on Oak Street? _____

4. Is the bank on Oak Street? _____

7B. Look at the map in 7A. Complete the sentences.

✔

across from   next to   on

1. The gas station is _____ on _____ Oak Street.

2. It's _____ the supermarket.

3. The bank is _____ the police station.

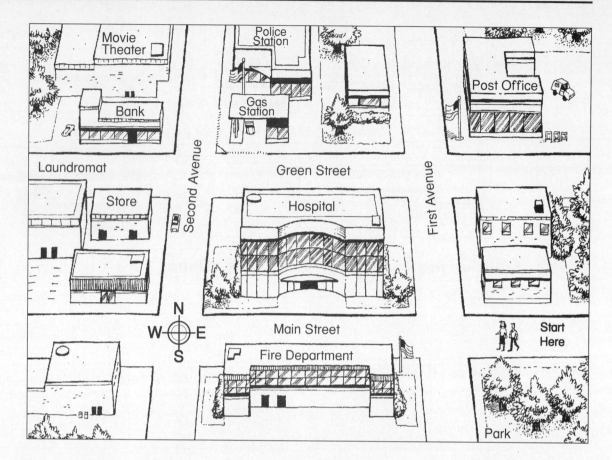

7C. Read the answers. Write the questions.

Where's the fire department?

➤ <u>Where's the police station?</u>
● The police station is on Second Avenue.

➤ _____
● The fire department is on Main Street, across from the hospital.

➤ _____
● The park is on the corner of Main Street and First Avenue.

Where do you want to go? Write three questions.

_____

_____

_____

**7 D. Complete the dialog.
Write *a* or *an*.**

an	accident
	emergency

a	hospital
	police car

1. This is __an__ emergency.

2. There's _____ accident at First Avenue and Elm Street.

3. There's _____ fire truck on Elm Street.

4. There's _____ ambulance on First Avenue.

5. There's _____ police car, too.

**8. Look at the map on page 14.
Complete the directions to the laundromat.**

✔

block	left	next to	right	west

1. Start at the park. Go ____west____ on Main Street.

2. Turn _____ on Second Avenue. Go one _____.

3. Turn _____. The laundromat is on the left.

4. It's _____ the store.

Write directions to the police station.

Start at the park. _____

_____

9. Ask for directions. Complete the dialog. ✔

next to   south   movie theater   where's

➤ <u>Where's</u> the _____?

● It's south of the hospital.

➤ Where?

● _____ of the hospital. It's on Second Avenue.

➤ How do I get there?

● Go south on Third Avenue. Turn right on Park Street.

Turn left on Second Avenue.

The movie theater is _____ the bank.

10. Complete the dialog. ✔

fire truck   phone   911

➤ Oh, no! A fire!

● Find a <u>phone</u>. Dial _____.

★ Oak City, 911.

➤ There's a fire in the park. Send a _____.

16

3 School and Country

I. Complete the sentences.

✔

| class   form   name   school   six   teacher |

1. How old is he? What _____class_____ is he in?

2. He's _____ years old.

3. His _____ is Minh.

4. Fill out the _____.

5. Then go and meet his _____ Kay.

6. Welcome to _____. Have a nice day.

2. What are they doing? Write the letters.

__c__	1. Binh, Alma, and Miguel	a.	is talking to his teacher.
_____	2. Anh	b.	is writing.
_____	3. Jesse	✔c.	are reading.

3. Complete the dialog.

✔

hall   me   room   secretary's   welcome

➤ Excuse _____me_____. Where's the _____ office?

● Go down the _____. Turn left.

The secretary's office is _____ 102.

➤ Thanks.

● You're _____.

4A. Write the words.

1. n o te b ook   2. d__or   3. __esk   4. p__n__il

4B. Find the words.

✔

CAFETERIA   CLASS   EXIT   HALL   OFFICE

N O X C B I T Q N (C L A S S)

S T I N X C H A L L Z P N E

C A F E T E R I A H C O N L

L C B E X I T R O F F I C E

R L E N M I K V A L Q U S E

4C. Look at the flag. Complete the sentences. Write the numbers.

The U.S. flag has _____50_____ stars.

The U.S. flag has _____ stripes.

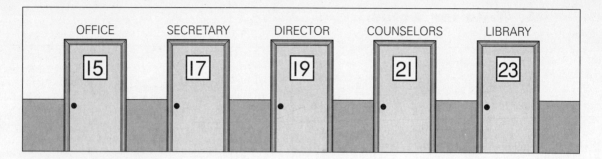

OFFICE	SECRETARY	DIRECTOR	COUNSELORS	LIBRARY
15	17	19	21	23

5. Complete the dialog.

✔

> office   15   19   23

➤ Excuse me. Where's the office?

● It's in room _____15_____.

➤ OK. Where's the director's _____?

● Room _____.

➤ Thanks. And the library?

● Room _____.

6. Look and read.

GATES TECHNICAL HIGH SCHOOL
CHICAGO, ILLINOIS 60657

NAME: Mei Wong

Math	A	She's doing excellent work.
English	B	Her English is improving a lot.
U.S. History	B	Mei can get an A if she works more.

Write yes or no.

yes   1. Mei Wong is getting the grade report.

_____   2. She can get an A in U.S. History if she works more.

_____   3. She's getting two C's.

7A. Write the correct form of the word on the line.

I'm		reading a book.
He's		
She's		
We're		
You're		
They're		

I'm not		reading a book.
He	isn't	
She		
We	aren't	
You		
They		

1. They <u>'re studying</u> (**study**) English

2. The teacher_____ (**meet**) a new student.

3. The secretary_____ (**not close**) the door.

7B. Complete the dialog.

Am	I	doing good work?
Is	he	
	she	
Are	we	
	you	
	they	

Yes,	you	are.
No,		aren't.

What	are you	doing?
Where		going?

➤ <u>Are</u> you _____<u>studying</u>_____ (**study**) math?

● No, I _____. I _____ (**study**) English.

➤ Oh. _____ Sylvia _____ (**study**) English, too?

● No, she _____.

➤ What _____ she _____ (**do**)?

● She _____ (**read**) a book about U.S. history.

7C. Write the word. Use 's or s'.

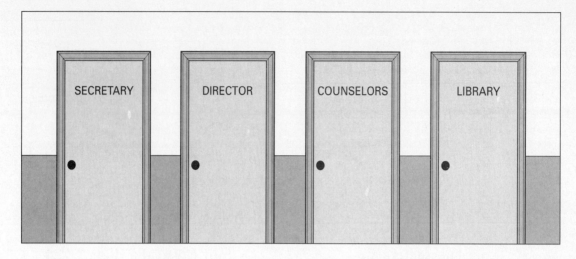

SECRETARY   DIRECTOR   COUNSELORS   LIBRARY

1. The _____secretary's_____ (secretary) office is down the hall.

2. It's next to the _____ (director) office.

3. The _____ (counselors) office is between the director's office and the library.

8. Complete the note. Write about yourself.

✔

| home   school   sick |

Dear _____,

                  (your teacher's name)

Please excuse me from ___school___.

I am _____.

I'm staying _____ today.

Thank you very much.

_____

(your signature)

9. You are going to the cafeteria. Ask for directions. Complete the dialog.

| around | down | Excuse | next to | 34 |

➤ <u>Excuse</u> me. Where's the cafeteria?

● Room _____.

➤ Room 34?

● Yes.

➤ How do I get there?

● Go _____ the corner and _____ the hall.

➤ Is it next to the library?

● No, it's _____ the office.

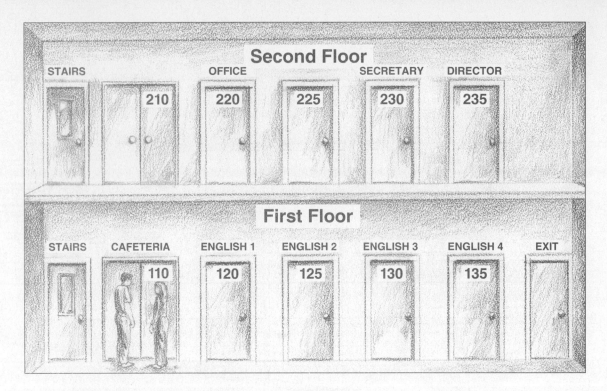

10. Complete the dialog. ✔

| floor   office   second   secretary's   stairs   230 |

➤ Excuse me. Where are you going?

● I'm going to the ___secretary's___ office.

➤ Oh. Where is the secretary's _____?

● Room _____.

➤ What _____ is it on?

● It's on the _____ floor. Go up the _____

and down the hall.

➤ Thanks.

Unit

4 Daily Living

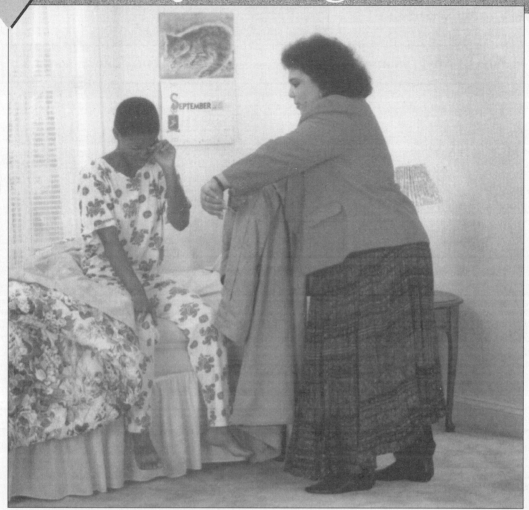

I. Complete the sentences.

| date late time twenty-first way |

1. What's the __date__ ?

2. September _____ .

3. Oh no! I'm _____ !

4. I have to be on _____ today.

5. Hurry up! Get on your _____ !

2. Look at the pictures.
What season is it? How's the weather?
Write the words.

✔

| fall   spring   summer   winter |

✔

| cold   cool   hot   warm |

1. _____fall_____

_____cool_____

2. _____

_____

3. _____

_____

4. _____

_____

3. Look at the clock. What time is it? Write the answer.

1. ___It's 7:00.___

2. _____

3. _____

4. _____

4A. Complete the chart about where you live. How's the weather? Write the words.

cold   cool   hot   warm

raining   snowing   sunny   windy

Fall	Winter	Summer	Spring
cool			

4B. Read the date. Look at the calendar. What day of the week is it?

```
              September
     S   M   T   W  TH   F   S
     1   2   3   4   5   6   7
     8   9  10  11  12  13  14
    15  16  17  18  19  20  21
    22  23  24  25  26  27  28
    29  30
```

1. September 1 = _____ Sunday _____

2. September 7 = _____

3. September 11 = _____

4. September 16 = _____

5. September 20 = _____

6. September 24 = _____

7. September 26 = _____

4C. Circle the months.

| ✔ JANUARY |
| FEBRUARY |
| APRIL |
| JUNE |
| SEPTEMBER |
| DECEMBER |

```
L  B  F  E  B  R  U  A  R  Y  M
M  Q  O  J  U  N  E  D  B  Y  P
J  A  N  U  A  R  Y  P  O  B  Y
Q  O  Y  L  T  V  A  P  R  I  L
W  T  D  E  C  E  M  B  E  R  L
S  E  P  T  E  M  B  E  R  K  M
```

5. Look and read.

Newburg News

WEATHER

High Low
92 85
Hot and sunny today.

MORNING EDITION   THURSDAY, JULY 7, 1994

Answer the questions about the newspaper.

1. What day is it?   It's Thursday.

2. What month is it?   _____

3. What's the date?   _____

4. How's the weather?   _____

6. Study the calendar pages. Answer the questions.

May						
S	**M**	**T**	**W**	**T**	**F**	**S**
1	2	3	4	5	6	7
8 Mother's Day	9	10	11	12	13	14
15	16	17	18	19	20	21
22	23	24	25	26	27	28
29	30 Memorial Day	31				

June						
S	**M**	**T**	**W**	**T**	**F**	**S**
			1	2	3	4
5	6	7	8	9	10	11
12	13	14 Flag Day	15	16	17	18
19 Father's Day	20	21	22	23	24	25
26	27	28	29	30		

1. When is Mother's Day?   May 8

2. When is Flag Day?   _____

3. What holiday is on a Monday?   _____

4. What two holidays are on Sundays? _____

7A. **Look at the picture. Read the answers.**
Write the questions.

What	month day season time	is it?

It's	May. Tuesday. spring. 10:00.

1. _____What season is it?_____ It's winter.

2. _____ It's December.

3. _____ It's Tuesday.

4. _____ It's 6:45.

7B. **Look at the pictures. Write about the weather.**

It's	raining. snowing.

It's	sunny. hot.

1. _It's sunny._   2. _____   3. _____   4. _____

7C. Look at the picture. Complete the sentences.

Is it	snowing?
	cold?
	January?
	winter?
	sunny?
	Saturday?

Yes,	it	is.
No,		isn't.

1. <u>Is it</u> summer?   No, <u>it isn't</u>.

2. _____ raining?   Yes, _____.

3. _____ May?   No, _____.

4. _____ windy?   Yes, _____.

8. Complete the form.

Date of Birth ___ / ___ / ___

Date ___ / ___ / ___

Signature _____

9. What's the date? What time is it?
Write the answers.

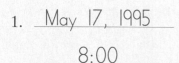

1. <u>May 17, 1995</u>

          <u>8:00</u>

2. _____

3. _____

10. Read the sign. Answer the questions.

1. What time does the store open on Monday?   <u>9:00</u>

2. What time does it open on Saturday?   _____

3. What time does it close on Saturday?   _____

4. What day is the store closed?   _____

5 Food

1. Complete the sentences. ✔

| aisle gallon pounds tea what |

1. Excuse me, please, I'm looking for _____tea_____.

2. It's on the top shelf in _____ number three.

3. _____ else do we need?

4. A _____ of milk, two _____ of steak.

2. Where do you find the food?
Draw a line to the supermarket section.

Food	Section
apples	bakery
milk	produce
ground beef	dairy
bread	meat

3. Complete the dialog.

> beef   onions   oranges   vegetables   want

➤ Let's shop for groceries. What do we _____want_____?

● Well, I want some vegetables.

➤ What kind of _____?

● Tomatoes, _____, and potatoes.

➤ Do we want any meat?

● Yes, ground _____ and chicken.

➤ How about some fruit?

● Yes. Let's get some apples and _____.

➤ OK.

4A. Look at the food. Write the words.

> apples   bread   carrots   cheese   chicken   eggs

1. ____apples____ 2. _____ 3. _____

4. _____ 5. _____ 6. _____

4B. Find the words.

> APPLES
> CHEESE
> GALLON
> LOAF
> ✔ MILK
> ORANGES

(M I L K) E L O A F

F G H I J B K L I

B R C H E E S E T

O A B C D P E F G

T L O R A N G E S

A P P L E S V W X

E Y Z G A L L O N

4C. What are these foods?
Write the missing letters.

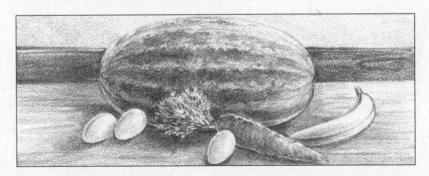

1. b a n a n a

2. c __ rr __ t

3. e __ __ s

4. w __ t __ rm __ l __ n

5. Look at the shopping list. Look at the picture. Answer the questions.

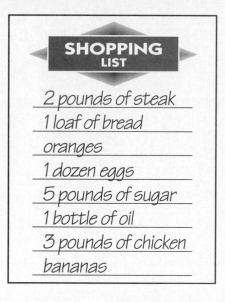

SHOPPING LIST

2 pounds of steak
1 loaf of bread
oranges
1 dozen eggs
5 pounds of sugar
1 bottle of oil
3 pounds of chicken
bananas

1. What did the people forget to buy?   chicken

2. What extra item did they buy?   _____

6. Read the questions. Circle the letter.

1. Today's date is 6/16. Which eggs will you buy?

a. 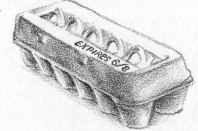   b.

2. Which milk will you buy?

a.    b.

7A. Complete the dialog. Write *a, an,* or *some.*

I want	a	potato.
	an	egg.
	some	eggs.
		potatoes.

I want some	lettuce.
	water.

➤ Let's make _____some_____ cookies.

● No, let's make _____ cake.

➤ OK. What's in the recipe?

● Well, let's look. It says we need _____ egg.

➤ And _____ milk, too.

● We have milk. Let's get _____ oil.

➤ Wait a minute. Let's make _____ shopping list.

7B. Complete the dialog. Write *how much* or *how many.*

How	much	lettuce water	do you want?
	many	eggs potatoes	

➤ Let's go shopping for food.

● OK. Let's make a list. What do we want?

➤ Tomatoes.

● <u>How many</u> tomatoes?

➤ Oh, three or four. What about sugar?

● Sugar, OK. _____ sugar?

➤ Five pounds. Let's buy some eggs.

● OK. _____ eggs?

➤ Let's get two dozen. Anything else?

● No.

➤ OK. Let's go!

8. Look at the food.
Write a shopping list.

SHOPPING LIST

Eggs _____ _____

_____ _____

_____ _____

_____ _____

9. **Look at the shopping list. Look at the food in the ad. Write the prices on the shopping list.**

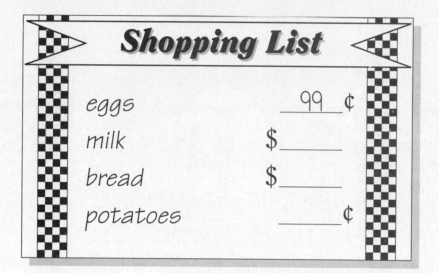

Shopping List

eggs   99 ¢

milk $ _____

bread $ _____

potatoes   _____ ¢

ACE SUPERMARKET

SALE!   SAVE!

Eggs   **Milk**   **Potatoes**   **Bread**
99¢ a dozen $1¹⁰ a gallon   89¢ a five-pound bag $1⁴⁹ a loaf

10. **Look at the pictures. Match the food and the packages.**

___c___ 1. apples   _____ 3. soy sauce

_____ 2. honey   _____ 4. spaghetti

a.   b.   ✔ c.   d.

6 Shopping

I. Complete the sentences.

✔

> blue   shirt   size   small   wear

1. What _____size_____ do you wear?

2. I wear a _____.

3. Do you want a coat to _____ this fall?

4. No. I'd like a shirt and I prefer _____.

5. This _____ is cotton. It'll fit you.

2. Complete the passage.

✔

> bathing suit   blue   sale   sneakers   summer   try on

It's ___summer___. Bathing suits and _____

are on _____.

Kate wants a new _____. Her favorite color

is _____.

She's going to _____ the blue bathing suit.

3. Complete the dialog.

✔

| color   much   shoes   size   try |

➤ Can I help you?

● Yes. I need a pair of ____shoes____.

➤ What _____ do you wear?

● Size 7.

➤ What _____ do you want?

● I like black. How _____ are these black shoes?

➤ $30.

● Great. I want to _____ them on.

4A. Find the words.

✔ BLACK
BLUE
BROWN
GRAY
GREEN
ORANGE
PINK
PURPLE
RED
WHITE
YELLOW

B L A C K G R A Y W T
J K G R E E N Q R E D
A O M T S K B U L C F
O R A N G E S T U V W
B L U E F P U R P L E
L P O R B E R T W A J
C D E Y E L L O W L M
W H I T E H B P I N K
F T B R O W N K A T H
R U V P N A H Y G I N

4B. What are they? Write the words.

✔

| dress hat jacket pants shirt shoes |
| shorts skirt socks suit sweater tie |

1. This is a <u>dress</u> .

2. This is a _____ .

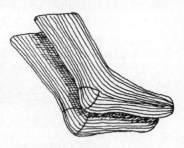

3. These are _____ .

4. This is a _____ .

5. This is a _____ .

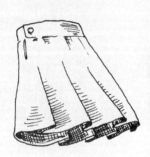

6. This is a _____ .

7. These are _____ .

8. This is a _____ .

9. These are _____ .

10. This is a _____ .

11. These are _____ .

12. This is a _____ .

4C. How much money is this? Write the amount.

1.

   $1.42

2.

   _____

3.

   _____

4.

   _____

5.

   _____

6.

   _____

4D. What are they? Match the word with its definition.

__b__   1. department store

____   2. cashier

____   3. dressing room

____   4. sales clerk

Definitions

a. the person who helps you find the clothes you want

b. where you can shop for clothes

c. where you try on the clothes

d. the person you pay for the clothes

5. Look at the clothes. Read the price tags. Complete the dialog.

➤ I'd like to pay for these clothes. How much are they?

● The bathing suit is on sale for ___$15.00___, and the

   shoes are _____ .

➤ How about the shorts and the T-shirt?

● The shorts are _____ , and the T-shirt is _____ .

6. Tamara's buying some clothes. This is her receipt. Look and read. Answer the questions.

```
              RECEIPT
dress ............................... $ 39.95
shorts .................................. 7.50
pants ................................. 19.95
shirt ................................... 5.60
Subtotal ............................. 73.00
Tax ..................................... 3.65
Total ................................. 76.65
Amt. paid ........................... 80.00
Change ................................ 3.35
```

1. What's the total cost of the items? $76.65

2. How much is the tax?   _____

3. How much money did Tamara give to the cashier?   _____

4. How much change did she get?   _____

7A. Rudy and Dana are shopping. Complete the dialog.

I want	this	shirt.
	that	

I want	these	shoes.
	those	

➤ Do you want to go in ___this___ (this, those) store?

● Yes. I want a suit for my job interview.

Oh, look at _____ (that, those) suits.

➤ I like _____ (that, these) blue suit.

● Yes, it's nice. I also like _____ (this, those) black suit.

➤ Me, too. I like _____ (this, these) shoes, too.

7B. A sales clerk is helping Marta find a sweater for her daughter. Complete the dialog.

What size	do	you	wear?
		they	
	does	he	
		she	

I	wear	size 8.
They		
He	wears	
She		

➤ What size ___does___ your daughter ___wear___ (wear)?

● She _____ (wear) a medium.

➤ How about this one? What color _____

your daughter _____ (like)?

● She _____ (like) blue. I _____ (like)

blue, too. Do you have those blue sweaters in my size?

➤ What size _____ you _____ (wear)?

● I _____ (wear) a large.

8. Write a check for $25.00 to Buy-Mart.
Print your name and address.
Print today's date. Sign your name.

604

_____

_____   19 ____

_____

PAY TO THE
ORDER OF _____ $ | 25.00 |

_____ DOLLARS

K Bank
200 Main St.
El Paso, TX 79912

_____

9061135

9. Mr. Jones wants new clothes. Look at the two ads.
Where should he buy his clothes? Circle the ad.

SAVE MART

SALE   SALE   SALE

Jeans   Shorts   Shoes
Only *$15.00*   Only *$10.99*   Only *$10.00*

SALE! SAVE!   Clothes Land

Jeans   Shorts   Shoes
$19.99 $12.99 $10.99

Two
Convenient
Locations

ALL MERCHANDISE 30%–50% OFF!

10. Read about the people. Use the chart. Write the people's sizes.

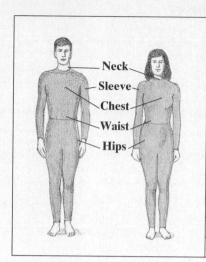

	WOMEN'S SIZES								
Size	P	S		M		L		XL	
	4	6	8	10	12	14	16	18	20
Chest	33	34	35	36	38	40	42	44	46
Waist	25	26	27	28	29	31	32	34	35
Hips	35	36	38	39	40	42	43	45	46

	MEN'S SIZES			
Size	S	M	L	XL
Neck	14–14 ½	15–15 ½	16–16 ½	17–17 ½
Chest	34–36	38–40	42–44	46–48
Waist	28–30	32–34	36–38	40–42
Sleeve	32–33	33–34	34–35	35–36

1. Mei's measurements are:
   Chest 34
   Waist 26
   Hips 36

   What size dress does she wear?

   Write the number. __6__

2. Arturo's measurements are:
   Neck 16
   Chest 44
   Waist 36
   Sleeve 35

   What size shirt does he wear?

   Write the letter. _____

3. Alma's measurements are:
   Chest 38
   Waist 29
   Hips 40
   What size blouse does she wear?

   Write the number. _____

4. Michael's measurements are:
   Neck 14 1/2
   Chest 35
   Waist 30
   What size sweater does he wear?

   Write the letter. _____

I. Complete the sentences.

✔

| carpet door floor owner plumber sink |

1. The kitchen _____sink_____ is broken.

2. There's water on the _____.

3. It's ruining the _____.

4. And running out the _____.

5. Let's call a _____ right away.

6. Let's call the _____, too!

2. Which room are these things in? Write the letter.

____c____ 1. sink and towels   a. living room

_____ 2. bed and dresser   b. kitchen

_____ 3. stove and refrigerator   ✔ c. bathroom

_____ 4. sofa and chair   d. bedroom

3. Complete the dialog.

✔

| apartment bathrooms bedroom dresser house sofa |

➤ I live in an _____apartment_____. Do you?

● No. I live in a _____.

➤ My apartment has one _____ and one bathroom. What's your house like?

● Well, it has two bedrooms and two _____.
I don't have much furniture. I want to buy a few things.

➤ Oh, really? What do you want to buy?

● Hmm. I'd like a _____ and a lamp for the living room.

➤ That sounds great! I want a _____ for my bedroom.

4A. Cross out the word that doesn't belong.

1. stove
   refrigerator
   ~~bed~~
   table

2. rent
   deposit
   utilities
   bedroom

3. bathtub
   sofa
   chair
   lamp

4. bed
   bathtub
   sink
   towels

4B. Look and read. Write the numbers.

1. one hundred   <u>   100   </u>

2. one thousand   <u>   </u>

3. eight hundred   <u>   </u>

4. three hundred   <u>   </u>

4C. Look at the pictures. Write the words.

                  ✔   ✔

coffee table   kitchen   lamp   living room   refrigerator   sink   sofa   stove

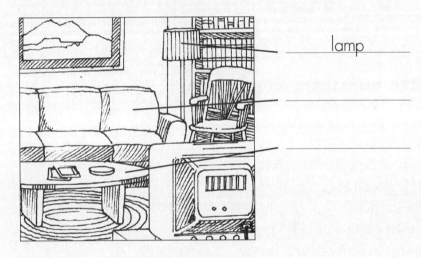

                                                  <u>lamp</u>

1. This is the <u>living room</u>.

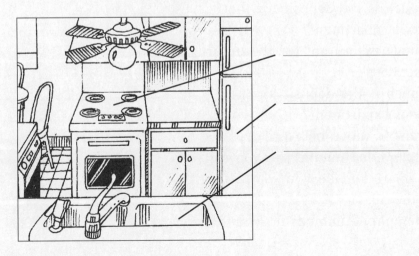

2. This is the <u>   </u>.

5. What do you do in these rooms? Circle the answer.

1. living room: (watch TV) wash dishes

2. kitchen: sleep cook

3. bathroom: cook take a bath

4. bedroom: sleep wash dishes

6. Look and read.

APTS FOR RENT

Apts Furnished
1 bdrm apt. Furn. $295 mo.
$100 deposit. No pets.
Call 555-8227. Available
May 1.

APTS FOR RENT

Apts Unfurnished
2 bdrm apt. Pets OK.
$310 mo. $200 deposit.
Call 555-2745, leave
message.

Answer the questions about the ads.

1. How much is the rent for the
   furnished apartment? _____ $295 _____

2. You want a 2-bedroom apartment.
   What telephone number do you call? _____

3. You have a pet.
   Which telephone number do you call? _____

4. How many bedrooms are in the
   unfurnished apartment? _____

5. How much is the deposit for the
   2-bedroom apartment? _____

6. How much is the rent for the unfurnished
   apartment? _____

7. How much is the deposit for the
   1-bedroom apartment? _____

8. You want to move on April 15.
   What telephone number do you call? _____

9. Which apartment do you want to rent?
   Circle the ad.
   What telephone number do you call? _____

7A. Write the question. Complete the answer.

How many	bedrooms	are there?
	bathrooms	

There	are	two bedrooms.
There's		one bathroom.

1. <u>How many bathrooms are there?</u>   <u>There are</u> two bathrooms.

2. _____   _____ one rug.

3. _____   _____ four lamps.

4. _____   _____ six windows.

7B. Complete the sentences.

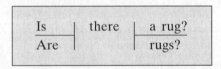

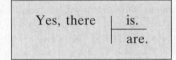

➤ Please tell me about the apartment you have for rent.

<u>Are there</u> _____ curtains for the windows?

● Yes, _____. There are curtains in every room.

➤ _____ a rug in the bedroom?

● No, _____. But there's a rug in the living room.

➤ I'd like to see the apartment. _____ a deposit?

● Yes, _____. It's $200.

7C. Look at the picture. Complete the sentences.

The chair is	in front of	the sofa.
	in back of	
	near	
	beside	

1. The chair is _____near_____ the sofa.

2. The picture is _____ the sofa.

3. The coffee table is _____ the sofa.

4. The lamp is _____ the sofa.

Write two sentences about the furniture in your home. Follow the examples above.

_____

_____

8. Look at the picture. What's the matter?

Complete the note to ask for repairs.

✔

| plumber   repairs   stopped   toilet |

Dear Ms. Vargas,

My apartment needs _____repairs_____.

The _____ is _____ up.

Please call a _____ right away.

Thank you very much.

Ricardo Zamora

9. Look and read. Use the ad to complete the dialog.

Apt for Rent	Apt for Rent	Apt for Rent
1802 South First Street.	235 Elm St.	637 Washington Avenue.
2 bdrm, 1 ba. Furn.	3 bdrm, 2 ba. furn.	Lg unfurn 1 bdrm, 1 ba.
$285 mo./$200 deposit.	$350 mo. $250 deposit.	$270 mo./$200 deposit.
Call 555-3607.	Call 555-0212 now!	Call 555-4532.

➤ How much is the rent at _____235 Elm Street_____?

● It's _____.

➤ How much is the _____?

● $250.

➤ How many bedrooms are there?

● There are _____ bedrooms.

➤ Is the apartment furnished or unfurnished?

● It's _____.

10. Luisa Villegas is calling about utilities for her new apartment. Complete the dialog.

✔

address   deposit   electricity   gas   mail

➤ Hello. South Bay Gas and Electric Company. How can I help you?

● My name is Luisa Villegas. I need the _____electricity_____ and

the _____ turned on in my apartment, please.

➤ What's your _____?

● 1092 First Street. Is there a deposit?

➤ Yes, there's a $100 _____.

You can pay it by _____.

8 Health Care

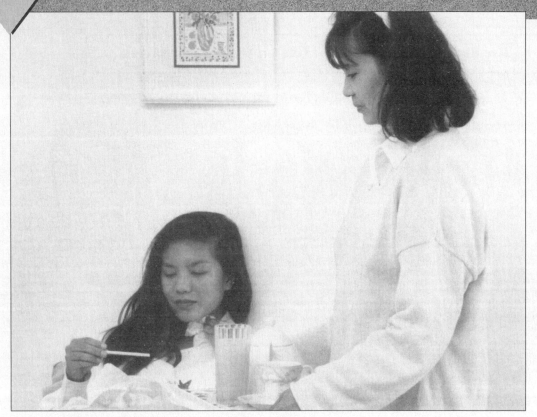

I. Complete the sentences.

✔

| bed feel flu rest |

1. I feel awful with this _____flu_____.

2. Stay in _____.

3. Get some _____.

4. And you'll _____ better soon.

2. Read the sentences. Write *yes* or *no*.

1. Go to the dentist for a stomachache. _____no_____

2. Go to the emergency room for a broken arm. _____

3. Go to the health clinic if you're pregnant. _____

4. Go to the hospital for a toothache. _____

3. Dawn is getting a check-up. Look at the pictures. What does the doctor tell her to do? Write the sentences.

✔

Breathe in.   Breathe out.   Get on the scale.   Say ah.

1. <u>Breathe in.</u>   2. _____   3. _____

4A. Find the words.

✔

| CLINIC |
| COLD |
| DENTIST |
| DOCTOR |
| FLU |
| HEADACHE |
| TOOTHACHE |

```
L F J M N U R R E N M T
H E A D A C H E M C O L
J B K M S S A M L B O K
U V N Y C L I N I C Y W
Y E U T N O F L U U I N
N M D O C T O R O P C U
T O O T H A C H E N M I
M N U G U N D E N X C T
N M G H I Z R C O L D Q
D E L H D E N T I S T O
```

4B. Look at the people. What's the matter?
Complete the sentences. ✔

cough earache foot head

1. Her ___head___ hurts.   2. His _____ hurts.   3. He has a _____.

4C. Look at the picture. Write the words. ✔

arm   chest   finger   foot   head   knee   leg   shoulder   stomach

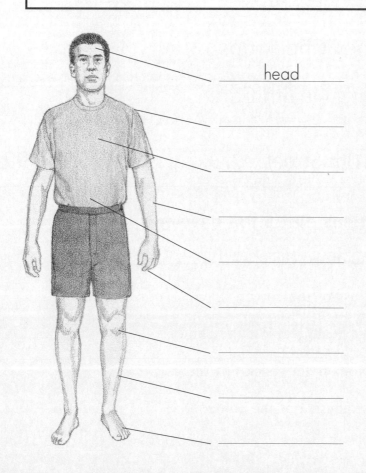

head

_____

_____

_____

_____

_____

_____

_____

5. Read the sentences. What should the people do? Write the letter.

<u>d</u> 1. Sharon has a cold.

_____ 2. Dao has a broken arm.

_____ 3. Rosa has the flu.

_____ 4. Mike has a toothache.

a. He needs to go to the emergency room.

b. She needs to go to the doctor.

c. He needs to see the dentist.

✔ d. She needs to get plenty of rest and drink water, tea, and juice.

6. Look and read.

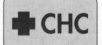 **CHC COMMUNITY HEALTH CLINIC**

Low cost health care for the whole family!

- General Check-ups

- Pregnancy Check-ups

- Children's Health Care

408 West 10th Street. **555–8924**

Read the questions. Write the answers.

1. What's the name of the clinic? <u>Community Health Clinic</u>

2. What's the address of the clinic? _____

3. Can children get health care at the clinic? _____

4. Can pregnant women get check-ups there? _____

5. Is health care expensive at the clinic? _____

7A. Complete the dialogs.

How	do	I	feel?
		we	
		you	
		they	
	does	he	
		she	

I	feel	sick.
We		
You		
They		
He	feels	
She		

1. ➤ How ___do___ you feel?

   ● I ___feel___ cold.

2. ➤ How _____ he feel?

   ● He _____ hot.

3. ➤ How _____ they feel?

   ● They _____ sick.

4. ➤ How _____ you feel?

   ● We _____ fine.

7B. Complete the dialog.

I	have	the flu.
We		
You		
They		
He	has	
She		

➤ Hi, Gustavo. How are you?

● I ___have___ a little cold. How are you?

➤ I'm fine, but Rita _____ the flu.

   She _____ a fever, and her head hurts.

● That's too bad. How are your children?

➤ They _____ the flu, too. Are your children OK?

● Oh, yes. They're fine.

8. You have a sore throat and a fever. You go to a new doctor. Complete the form. Write about yourself.

 County Clinic

PATIENT INFORMATION FORM

Name _____

Address _____

Telephone Number _____ Date of Birth _____

Who can we call in an emergency?

Name _____

Telephone Number _____

What are your symptoms? Check here (✓).

_____ backache

_____ cough

_____ earache

_____ fever

_____ headache

_____ sore throat

_____ stomachache

Are you pregnant? _____

Do you take any medicine? _____

Signature _____ Date _____

9. Look at the people. What's the matter?
Complete the sentences.

| backache | cold | fever | sore throat | stomachache | toothache | ✔ |

1. He has a ___toothache___ .   2. She has a _____ .

3. She has a _____ .   4. He has a _____ .

5. He has a _____ .   6. She has a _____ .

10. Study the thermometers. Answer the questions.

Normal Temperature

Linda's Temperature

1. What's normal temperature? _____98.6_____ degrees

2. What's Linda's temperature? _____ degrees

3. Does Linda have a fever? _____

Complete the dialog. ✔

| appointment headache matter morning temperature |

➤ Good morning. Dr. Ortega's office.

● Good morning. This is Linda Crain. I need

to make an _____appointment_____.

➤ What's the _____?

● I have a _____ and a high fever.

➤ What's your _____?

● 102 degrees.

➤ Can you come in this _____ at 11:30?

● Yes, I can.

➤ OK, Ms. Crain. The doctor will see you then.

Unit 9

Employment

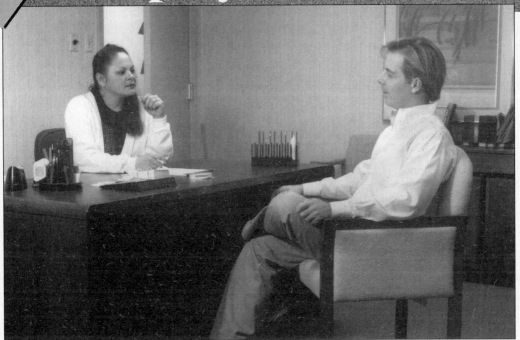

I. Complete the sentences.

> can   cars   drive   job

1. What _____can_____ you do?

2. I can _____ a cab.

3. And fix _____, too.

4. Then I can find a _____ for you.

2. Pedro is interviewing for a job. Complete the dialog.

> long   paint   painter   23

➤ Can you _____paint_____ houses, Pedro?

● Yes, I can. I was a _____ in my country.

➤ How _____ were you a painter?

● For _____ years.

Unit 9   65

3. Complete the sentences. ✔

clean   cook   fix   grow   paint

1. Painters _____paint_____ houses.

2. Housekeepers _____ houses.

3. Mechanics _____ cars.

4. Gardeners _____ plants.

5. Cooks _____ food.

4A. Look at the pictures. Write the words. ✔

child care worker   gardener   mechanic   plumber

1. ____child care worker____

2. _____

3. _____

4. _____

4B. Find the words.

✔
| APPLICATION |
| COMPANY |
| EXPERIENCE |
| INTERVIEW |
| JOB |
| WORK |

```
U E X P E R I E N C E B
J R V U C A L P X K I L
E J O B N C E Q I J P S
F G D S L W U O Y F X U
L Y Y W X C O M P A N Y
I N T E R V I E W F E R
U A P P L I C A T I O N
U A I G D F S P M J O L
J U V O B M U W Y E X P
I N T W O R K C A Q P J
```

4C. Unscramble the letters. Write the words.

✔
| cook   driver   gardener   housekeeper   painter |

1. koco _____cook_____

2. perhokeeuse _____

3. taepirn _____

4. vedrir _____

5. energrad _____

4D. What can you do? What job do you want? Complete the sentences. Write about yourself.

I can _____.

I want to be _____.

5. Read about Janet Sandoval's work experience.

WORK EXPERIENCE

Job _____cook_____   Employer _____Joe's Restaurant_____

How long were you at this job? _____3 years_____

Job _____housekeeper_____   Employer _____Jean Belton_____

How long were you at this job? _____2 years_____

Answer the questions.

1. What were Janet's jobs?   _____cook_____ and _____

2 How long was she a cook?   _____

3. How long was she a housekeeper?   _____

6. Look and read.

HELP WANTED

Housekeeper wanted.	PAINTER WANTED.	Wanted: Experienced
Evenings. Apply in person at 1129 Park St. Monday to Friday 8 to 5.	No experience necessary. Call for an interview, 555-0713.	Gardener. Call for an appointment. 555-6329, Monday only.

Answer the questions.

1. When can you apply for the housekeeper's job?   _____Monday to Friday 8 to 5_____

2. Do you need experience for the painter's job?   _____

3. What telephone number do you call for the gardener's job?   _____

4. Do you have to apply in person for the housekeeper's job?   _____

5. Do you need experience for the gardener's job?   _____

7A. Complete the dialogs. Write *can* or *can't*.

What can	I	do?
	you	
	he	
	she	
	we	
	they	

I	can	drive a bus.
He	can't	
She		
We		
You		
They		

Can	I	drive a bus?
	he	
	she	
	we	
	you	
	they	

Yes,	I	can.
No,		can't.

1.

➤ Hello. I'm looking for a job.

● What _____can_____ you do?

➤ I _____ cook. I _____ clean houses, too.

● _____ you drive a car?

➤ No, I _____. But I _____ learn.

● Great! Then I _____ find a job for you.

➤ Thank you.

2.

➤ Hello. _____Can_____ I help you?

● Yes. I want a job.

➤ What _____ you do?

● I _____ grow plants.

7B. Complete the dialog.

I	was	a cook.
He		
She		
You	were	

We	were	cooks.
You		
They		

➤ What did you do in your country, Sonia?

● I _____was_____ a cook. What did you do, Pedro?

➤ I _____ a farmer. I _____ a gardener, too.

● Ana and Arturo _____ painters in their country.

They paint houses here, too.

7C. Complete the dialog. Write *from, for,* or *how long.*

How long were you a cook?

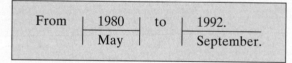

From	1980	to	1992.		For	twelve years.
	May		September.			four months.

➤ Mr. Arroyo, _____how long_____ were you a cook?

● _____ 1990 to 1992.

➤ And I see that you were also a gardener.

_____ were you a gardener?

● _____ three years. _____ 1987 to 1990.

Before that, I was a housekeeper _____ 1980 to 1987.

➤ Oh. _____ seven years?

● Yes, _____ almost seven years.

70

8. Complete the job application. Write about yourself.

Townsend Computer Corp.

3440 N. National Road, Great Hills, TX 79711

Application For Employment

PERSONAL INFORMATION ─────────────────

Name _____

Address _____

_____

Telephone _____ Social Security Number _____

WORK EXPERIENCE ─────────────────

Job _____ Employer _____

How long were you at this job? _____

_____

Job _____ Employer _____

How long were you at this job? _____

READ AND SIGN ─────────────────

The above information is true and correct.

_____   _____
Signature   Date

9. These people need jobs. Which ad should they answer? Write the letters.

HELP WANTED

(A.) **Lin's Garage needs a** mechanic immediately. Experience necessary. Call 555-4355.

(B.) **HOUSEKEEPER WANTED.** No experience necessary. Call 555-1832 for an appointment.

(C.) **GARDENER NEEDED** 3 years experience necessary. Apply at Green Thumb Gardeners, 279 Oak Street.

(D.) **Wanted: Experienced Plumber** Apply in person at Vale's Plumbing, 311 Main Street. Monday to Friday, 8 to 4.

_c_ 1. Lim-sing was a gardener for four years.

____ 2. Victor was a plumber for nine years.

____ 3. Alma was a housekeeper for six months.

____ 4. Samuel was a mechanic for seven years.

10. Look at the signs. What do they mean? Write the warnings.

✔

| Hard Hat Area   Keep Out   No Smoking |

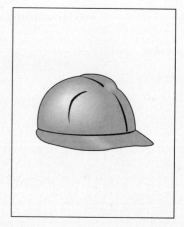

1. ___Keep out___

2. _____

3. _____

Transportation and Travel

I. Complete the sentences.

✔

fares   nation   reservation   travel

1. Ask for schedules, ask for _____fares_____.

2. Make a _____.

3. You can _____ near or far.

4. All across the _____.

2. Look at the pictures. Write the words.

1. s_u_bw_a_y

2. c__r

3. b__s

3. Complete the dialog.

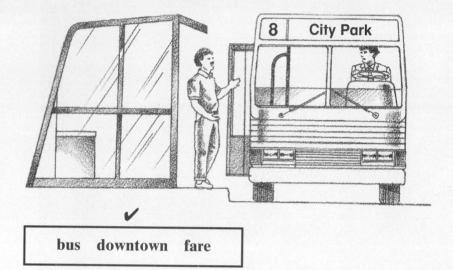

bus downtown fare

➤ Excuse me. Does this bus go _____downtown_____?

● No, it doesn't. Take _____ number 15.

➤ How much is the _____?

● It's $1.

4A. What are they? Match the word with its definition.

__d__ 1. driver's license

_____ 2. car pool

_____ 3. fare

_____ 4. station

a. train or subway stop

b. a group of people who drive to work together

c. the money you pay to ride the bus or train

d. what you need to drive a car

4B. Look at the picture. Complete the sentences.

caution go slow stop

1. The red light means _____stop_____.

2. The yellow light means drive with

_____ or _____ down.

3. The green light means _____.

RED

YELLOW

GREEN

4C. Look at the pictures. What are they? Write the words in the puzzle.

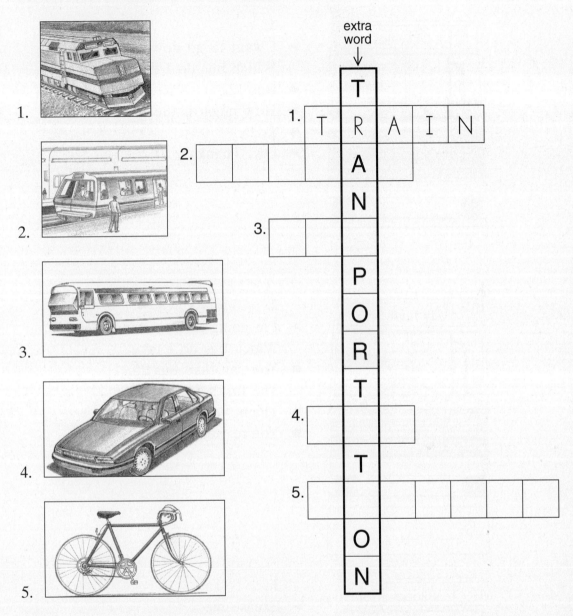

extra
word
↓

1.

2.

3.

4.

5.

1. T R A I N

2.

3.

4.

5.

(extra word column: T R A N P O R T T O N)

What extra word did you spell?

Write the word here. _____

5. Read the dialogs.
Write the bus numbers and the fares in the pictures.

$ \underline{1} . \underline{2} \ \underline{5}$

1.

➤ I want to go downtown.
   Which bus do I take?
● Bus 12.
➤ How much is the fare?
● $1.25.
➤ OK. Thanks.

$ \underline{\ \ } . \underline{\ \ } \ \underline{\ \ }$

2.

➤ I'm going to City Adult School.
   Which bus do I take?
● You can take bus 25.
   The fare's $1.50.
➤ Thank you.
● You're welcome.

$ \underline{\ \ } . \underline{\ \ } \ \underline{\ \ }$

3.

➤ Excuse me.
   Which bus is this?
● This is bus 30.
➤ Oh, good.
   What's the fare?
● $1.75.
➤ Thanks.

6. Match the sentence with the correct sign. Draw a line.

a.

1. Don't cross the street now.

b.

2. You can't turn around here.

c.

3. Don't drive faster than
   25 miles per hour.

d.

4. There's a hospital near here.

e.

5. This is where you catch the bus.

f.

6. You can't park your car here.

7A. Complete the sentences. Write about yourself.

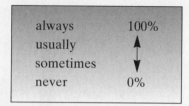

always	100%
usually	↑
sometimes	↓
never	0%

I always go to the park on Sunday.

1. I always _____ .

2. I usually _____ .

3. I sometimes _____ .

4. I never _____ .

7B. Complete the sentences.
Write the correct form of the word.

I always go to the bank on Friday.

I'm going to the bank right now.

1. I'm ___going___ (go) shopping right now.

2. I usually _____ (walk) to the store.

3. I sometimes _____ (take) the bus.

4. But right now, it's _____ (rain).

5. My sister _____ (drive) me to the store.

7C. Complete the dialogs. Use the bus signs.
Write the questions.

Which bus do I take?

➤ <u>Which bus do I take to the train station?</u>

● Bus 13.

➤ _____

● Bus 4.

➤ _____

● Bus 66.

8. How do you get from school to home? Write directions.

_____

_____

_____

_____

_____

_____

_____

_____

9. Someone is at City Airport asking about bus routes. Use the bus route map to complete the dialog.

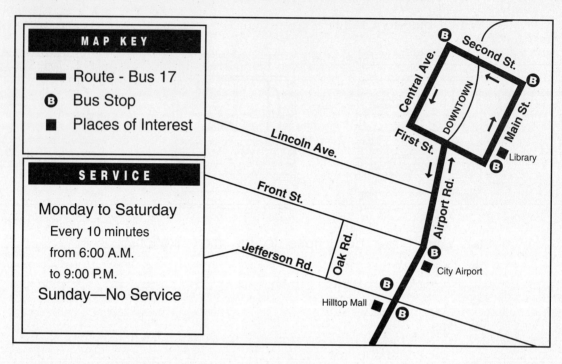

MAP KEY

━━━ Route - Bus 17
Ⓑ Bus Stop
■ Places of Interest

SERVICE

Monday to Saturday
Every 10 minutes
from 6:00 A.M.
to 9:00 P.M.
Sunday—No Service

➤ Excuse me. I want to go downtown. Which ____bus____ do I take?

● Bus number _____.

➤ Where do I catch it?

● At Front Street and _____ Road.

➤ OK. Does that bus go to Central Avenue?

● _____, it does.

10. Look at the bus route map and the bus schedule in 9. Read the sentences. Write *yes* or *no*.

____yes____ 1. You can catch bus 17 at Front Street and Airport Road.

_____ 2. Bus 17 stops at Lincoln Avenue and Airport Road.

_____ 3. You can take bus 17 to the library.

_____ 4. You can get from the airport to the corner of Central Avenue and First Street.

_____ 5. You can take bus 17 on Sunday.

Answer Key

Unit 1

Exercise 1 (Page 1)
2. last
3. from
4. you

Exercise 2 (Page 1)
Answers will vary.

Exercise 3 (Page 2)
Nice
meet
from
language
speak

Exercise 4A (Page 2)
2. two
3. three
4. nine
5. four
6. one

Exercise 4B (Page 3)

```
A D R G Y H E W T (N A M E) T
(N A T I O N A L I T Y) E T W
V E (S T A T E) R Y (C I T Y) I
X S R T G Q S T U K I U Y D
S A W (A D D R E S S) Q R T H
```

Exercise 4C (Page 3)
2. a
3. d
4. c

Exercise 4D (Page 3)
Answers will vary.

Exercise 5 (Page 4)
2. Maria
3. 123 Green Street, Los Angeles, CA
4. 91251
5. Mexico

Exercise 6 (Page 4)
3. no
4. no
5. no
6. yes

Exercise 7A (Page 5)
2. is, am
3. are, are
4. is, is
5. is, is
6. is, is

Exercise 7B (Page 5)
2. We're
3. She's
4. You're
5. He's
6. I'm

Exercise 7C (Page 6)
2. Her
3. Our
4. Our, Her
5. Their, His

Exercise 7D (Page 7)
What's your address?
What's your ZIP Code?
Where are you from?

Exercise 8 (Page 7)

Answers will vary.

Exercise 9 (Page 8)

Questions will vary.

Exercise 10 (Page 8)

you

Fine

see

Nice

Unit 2

Exercise 1 (Page 9)

supermarket

left

Exercise 2 (Page 9)

2. d

3. a

4. c

Exercise 3 (Page 10)

south

Street

post office

Avenue

across

Exercise 4A (Page 11)

2. p<u>o</u>st <u>o</u>ffice

3. f<u>i</u>re tr<u>u</u>ck

4. st<u>o</u>re

5. p<u>o</u>lice c<u>a</u>r

6. f<u>i</u>re

Exercise 4B (Page 11)

Turn

west

right

north

left

Exercise 5 (Page 12)

Street

next to

Exercise 6 (Page 12)

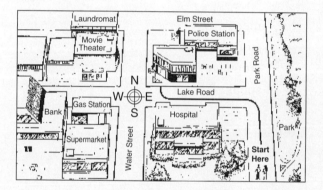

Exercise 7A (Page 13)

2. Yes, it is.

3. Yes, they are.

4. Yes, it is.

Exercise 7B (Page 13)

2. across from

3. next to

Exercise 7C (Page 14)

Where's the fire department?

Where's the park?

Questions will vary.

Exercise 7D (Page 15)

    2. an

    3. a

    4. an

    5. a

Exercise 8 (Page 15)

    2. right, block

    3. left

    4. next to

Directions to the police station will vary.

Exercise 9 (Page 16)

    movie theater

    South

    next to

Exercise 10 (Page 16)

    911

    fire truck

Unit 3

Exercise 1 (Page 17)

    2. six

    3. name

    4. form

    5. teacher

    6. school

Exercise 2 (Page 18)

    2. a

    3. b

Exercise 3 (Page 18)

    secretary's

    hall

    room

    welcome

Exercise 4A (Page 19)

    2. d<u>oo</u>r

    3. <u>d</u>esk

    4. p<u>e</u>n<u>c</u>il

Exercise 4B (Page 19)

```
N  O  X  C  B  I  T  Q  N (C  L  A  S  S)
S  T  I  N  X  C (H  A  L  L) Z  P  N  E
(C  A  F  E  T  E  R  I  A) H  C  O  N  L
L  C  B (E  X  I  T) R (O  F  F  I  C  E)
R  L  E  N  M  I  K  V  A  L  Q  U  S  E
```

Exercise 4C (Page 19)

    13

Exercise 5 (Page 20)

    office

    19

    23

Exercise 6 (Page 20)

    2. yes

    3. no

Exercise 7A (Page 21)

    2. 's meeting

    3. isn't closing

Exercise 7B (Page 21)

    'm not, 'm studying

    Is, studying

    isn't

    's, doing

    's reading

Exercise 7C (Page 22)

    2. director's

    3. counselors'

Exercise 8 (Page 22)

sick

home

Exercise 9 (Page 23)

34

around, down

next to

Exercise 10 (Page 24)

office

230

floor

second, stairs

Unit 4

Exercise 1 (Page 25)

2. twenty-first
3. late
4. time
5. way

Exercise 2 (Page 26)

2. winter
    cold
3. spring
    warm
4. summer
    hot

Exercise 3 (Page 27)

2. It's 6:30.
3. It's 3:15.
4. It's 4:00.

Exercise 4A (Page 27)

Answers will vary.

Exercise 4B (Page 28)

2. Saturday
3. Wednesday
4. Monday
5. Friday
6. Tuesday
7. Thursday

Exercise 4C (Page 28)

```
L  B  F  E  B  R  U  A  R  Y  M
M  Q  O  J  U  N  E  D  B  Y  P
J  A  N  U  A  R  Y  P  O  B  Y
Q  O  Y  L  T  V  A  P  R  I  L
W  T  D  E  C  E  M  B  E  R  L
S  E  P  T  E  M  B  E  R  K  M
```

Exercise 5 (Page 29)

2. It's July.
3. It's July 7, 1994.
4. It's hot and sunny.

Exercise 6 (Page 29)

2. June 14
3. Memorial Day
4. Mother's Day and Father's Day

Exercise 7A (Page 30)

2. What month is it?
3. What day is it?
4. What time is it?

Exercise 7B (Page 30)

2. It's snowing.
3. It's windy.
4. It's raining.

Exercise 7C (Page 31)
2. Is it, it is
3. Is it, it isn't
4. Is it, it is

Exercise 8 (Page 31)
Answers will vary.

Exercise 9 (Page 32)
2. August 12, 1995
   10:15
3. December 24, 1995
   7:45

Exercise 10 (Page 32)
2. 10:00
3. 5:00
4. Sunday

Unit 5

Exercise 1 (Page 33)
2. aisle
3. What
4. gallon, pounds

Exercise 2 (Page 33)

Food	Section
apples	bakery
milk	produce
ground beef	dairy
bread	meat

Exercise 3 (Page 34)
vegetables
onions
beef
oranges

Exercise 4A (Page 34)
2. bread
3. chicken
4. cheese
5. eggs
6. carrots

Exercise 4B (Page 35)

```
M I L K E L O A F
F G H I J B K L I
B R C H E E S E T
O A B C D P E F G
T L O R A N G E S
A P P L E S V W X
E Y Z G A L L O N
```

Exercise 4C (Page 35)
2. carrot
3. eggs
4. watermelon

Exercise 5 (Page 36)
1. bananas
2. apples

Exercise 6 (Page 36)
1. b
2. a

Exercise 7A (Page 37)
a
an
some
some
a

Exercise 7B (Page 38)
How much
How many

85

Exercise 8 (Page 39)

milk

bananas

cheese

grapes

rice

potatoes

carrots

Exercise 9 (Page 40)

$1.10

$1.49

89¢

Exercise 10 (Page 40)

2. b

3. d

4. a

Unit 6

Exercise 1 (Page 41)

2. small

3. wear

4. blue

5. shirt

Exercise 2 (Page 41)

sneakers, sale

bathing suit, blue

try on

Exercise 3 (Page 42)

size

color

much

try

Exercise 4A (Page 42)

```
B L A C K  G R A Y  W T
J K  G R E E N  Q  R E D
A O M T S K B U L C F
O R A N G E  S T U V W
B L U E  F  P U R P L E
L P O R B E R T W A J
C D E  Y E L L O W  L M
W H I T E  H B  P I N K
F T  B R O W N  K A T H
R U V P N A H Y G I N
```

Exercise 4B (Page 43)

2. shirt

3. socks

4. tie

5. jacket

6. skirt

7. shoes

8. suit

9. shorts

10. sweater

11. pants

12. hat

Exercise 4C (Page 44)

2. $6.50

3. $20.35

4. $15.30

5. $25.11

6. $40.75

Exercise 4D (Page 44)

2. d

3. c

4. a

86

Exercise 5 (Page 45)

$7.50

$5.00, $6.00

Exercise 6 (Page 45)

2. $3.65

3. $80.00

4. $3.35

Exercise 7A (Page 46)

those

that

this

these

Exercise 7B (Page 46)

wears

does, like

likes, like

do, wear

wear

Exercise 8 (Page 47)

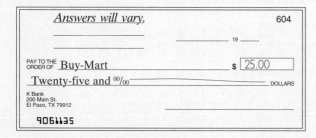

Exercise 9 (Page 47)

The ad for Save Mart should be circled.

Exercise 10 (Page 48)

2. L

3. 12

4. S

Unit 7

Exercise 1 (Page 49)

2. floor

3. carpet

4. door

5. plumber

6. owner

Exercise 2 (Page 49)

2. d

3. b

4. a

Exercise 3 (Page 50)

house

bedroom

bathrooms

sofa

dresser

Exercise 4A (Page 50)

2. bedroom

3. bathtub

4. bed

Exercise 4B (Page 51)

2. 1000

3. 800

4. 300

Exercise 4C (Page 51)

1. sofa, coffee table

2. kitchen, stove, refrigerator, sink

Exercise 5 (Page 52)

2. cook

3. take a bath

4. sleep

Exercise 6 (Page 52)

2. 555-2745
3. 555-2745
4. two
5. $200
6. $310
7. $100
8. 555–2745
9. *Answers will vary.*

Exercise 7A (Page 53)

2. How many rugs are there?
   There's
3. How many lamps are there?
   There are
4. How many windows are there?
   There are

Exercise 7B (Page 53)

there are
Is there
there isn't
Is there
there is

Exercise 7C (Page 54)

2. in back of
3. in front of
4. beside
Answers will vary.

Exercise 8 (Page 55)

toilet, stopped
plumber

Exercise 9 (Page 56)

$350
deposit
three
furnished

Exercise 10 (Page 56)

gas
address
deposit
mail

Unit 8

Exercise 1 (Page 57)

2. bed
3. rest
4. feel

Exercise 2 (Page 57)

2. yes
3. yes
4. no

Exercise 3 (Page 58)

2. Breathe out.
3. Say ah.

Exercise 4A (Page 58)

```
L F J M N U R R E N M T
H E A D A C H E M C O L
J B K M S S A M L B O K
U V N Y C L I N I C Y W
Y E U T N O F L U U I N
N M D O C T O R O P C U
T O O T H A C H E N M I
M N U G U N D E N X C T
N M G H I Z R C O L D Q
D E L H D E N T I S T O
```

Exercise 4B (Page 59)

2. foot
3. cough

88

Exercise 4C (Page 59)

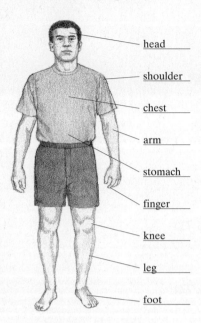

head
shoulder
chest
arm
stomach
finger
knee
leg
foot

Exercise 5 (Page 60)

2. a
3. b
4. c

Exercise 6 (Page 60)

2. 408 West 10th Street
3. yes
4. yes
5. no

Exercise 7A (Page 61)

2. does, feels
3. do, feel
4. do, feel

Exercise 7B (Page 61)

has, has
have

Exercise 8 (Page 62)

Sore throat *and* fever *should be checked. Other answers will vary.*

Exercise 9 (Page 63)

2. sore throat
3. cold
4. backache
5. fever
6. stomachache

Exercise 10 (Page 64)

2. 102 degrees
3. yes
matter
headache
temperature
morning

Unit 9

Exercise 1 (Page 65)

2. drive
3. cars
4. job

Exercise 2 (Page 65)

painter
long
23

Exercise 3 (Page 66)

2. clean
3. fix
4. grow
5. cook

Exercise 4A (Page 66)

2. plumber
3. mechanic
4. gardener

Exercise 4B (Page 67)

```
U (E X P E R I E N C E) B
J  R  V  U  C  A  L  P  X  K  I  L
E (J O B) N  C  E  Q  I  J  P  S
F  G  D  S  L  W  U  O  Y  F  X  U
L  Y  Y  W  X (C O M P A N Y)
(I N T E R V I E W) F  E  R
U (A P P L I C A T I O N)
U  A  I  G  D  F  S  P  M  J  O  L
J  U  V  O  B  M  U  W  Y  E  X  P
V  L  C  S  K  I  L  L  Y  X  K  A
I  N  T (W O R K) C  A  Q  P  J
```

Exercise 4C (Page 67)

2. housekeeper
3. painter
4. driver
5. gardener

Exercise 4D (Page 67)

Answers will vary.

Exercise 5 (Page 68)

1. housekeeper
2. 3 years
3. 2 years

Exercise 6 (Page 68)

2. no
3. 555-6329
4. yes
5. yes

Exercise 7A (Page 69)

1. can, can
   Can
   can't, can
   can
2. can
   can

Exercise 7B (Page 70)

was, was
were

Exercise 7C (Page 70)

From
How long
For, From, from
for
for

Exercise 8 (Page 71)

Answers will vary.

Exercise 9 (Page 72)

2. D
3. B
4. A

Exercise 10 (Page 72)

2. No Smoking
3. Hard Hat Area

Unit 10

Exercise 1 (Page 73)

2. reservation
3. travel
4. nation

Exercise 2 (Page 73)

2. c<u>a</u>r
3. b<u>u</u>s

Exercise 3 (Page 74)

bus
fare

Exercise 4A (Page 74)

    2. b

    3. c

    4. a

Exercise 4B (Page 74)

    2. caution, slow

    3. go

Exercise 4C (Page 75)

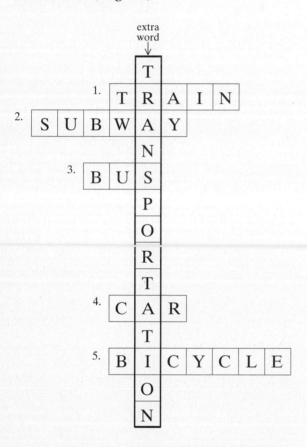

Extra word: TRANSPORTATION

Exercise 5 (Page 76)

    2. 25, $1.50

    3. 30, $1.75

Exercise 6 (Page 77)

    2. e

    3. b

    4. a

    5. f

    6. d

Exercise 7A (Page 78)

Answers will vary.

Exercise 7B (Page 78)

    2. walk

    3. take

    4. raining

    5. is driving

Exercise 7C (Page 79)

Which bus do I take to City Hall?
Which bus do I take to the library?

Exercise 8 (Page 79)

Answers will vary.

Exercise 9 (Page 80)

17
Airport
Yes

Exercise 10 (Page 80)

    2. no

    3. yes

    4. no

    5. no